Learning to Pray:

a book of longing

# Learning to Pray:

## a book of longing

New & Selected Poems & Aphorisms

Yahia Lababidi

Cover design by Shay Culligan
Cover photograph by Hasan Açan

ISBN: 978-1-63980-059-9

Kelsay Books
502 South 1040 East, A-119
American Fork, Utah 84003
Kelsaybooks.com

# Acknowledgments

With much gratitude to the fine publishers of the following journals and books where my poems and aphorisms appear:

*Balancing Acts* (Press 53, 2016): "Start, Again," "What the Sunset Said," "Hope," "Misread Signs," "Starlings," "Oceanside Epiphany," "Resting Place," "Gradual Escape," "Gestation"

*Barely There* (Wipf and Stock, 2013): "St. Sebastian," "Reaching," "Two of Us," "Taut," "Since," "Transportation," "Kneeling in Stages," "Mystery of Doors," "Morning," "Allegiances"

*Fair Observer:* "The Light-Keepers"

*Fever Dreams* (Crisis Chronicles Press, 2011): "Words," "The Art of Storm-Riding," "Dawning," "Interstices," "Unentitled," "Mystic, Misfit," "Drylands," "Afterthought," "Truth in Advertising," "I Saw My Face," "Turning on Faucet," "Poet Try," "You, Again," "Learning to Pray," "Poy," "Desert Revisited"

*Parabola:* "Summary"

*The Punch:* "Awakening from a Dream," "Two Types of Kisses," "Holy Mess"

*Queen Mob's Teahouse:* "What the Migraine Said," "Secrets," "11th Hour Plea," "Bargaining with Whom?"

*Signposts to Elsewhere* (Hay House, 2019): "Aphorisms"

*Torch* (University of Oxford): "Corona Verses," "Never Retreating"

# Contents

Aphorisms

*Only a little of life is left and you stand on the verge of a great voyage, all your knowledge and deeds are nothing but sham and pretense.*

—Abu Hamid al-Ghazali

# Preface

*Poetry is How We Pray, Now*

The human heart abhors a vacuum. With organized religion losing ground, all sorts of substitutes rush in to fill the God-shaped hole. One particularly effective and time-honored balm for the aching human heart is literature. For some, poetry is how we pray now.

In these skeptical times, there still exists an Absolute Literature, in the coinage of Italian writer Roberto Calasso, where we might discern the Divine Voice. Such pre- and post-religious literature share aims and concerns similar to belief systems: sharpening our attention, cultivating a sense of awe, offering us examples of how to better live and die—even granting us a chance at transcendence.

Mysteriously, certain strains of literary art are capable of using words to lose words—ushering us to the threshold of that quiet capital of riches: Silence. After all, it is in silent contemplation that difficulties patiently unfurl and entrust us with their secrets.

By deepening our silences, such literature allows us to overhear ourselves and can lend us a third (metaphysical) eye. We are able not only to bear witness to the here and now but, past that, calmly gaze at eternal things…over the head of our troubled times in order to try and understand our spiritual condition (where we've come from and where we're heading).

In our fractured world, beset by so much physical suffering and political turmoil, as a kind of (unconscious?) corrective, more people are reading and writing literature that addresses the life of the spirit, overtly or otherwise.

One manifestation of this renewed spiritual hunger that is being met by literature was the publication of a major anthology, *The Poet's Quest for God: 21ˢᵗ Century Poems of Faith, Doubt, and Wonder* (Eyewear, 2016), featuring over three hundred contemporary poets from around the world and of great value (as the jacket blurb indicates) "to those for whom poetry has become a resource or replacement for faith-bound spirituality." This ambitious book of collective soul-searching was followed by another similar anthology, *Without a Doubt: poems illustrating faith* (New York Quarterly, 2021). I'm fortunate to say that my prayer poems were featured in both these literary hymn books.

Likewise, more spiritual oases are appearing in the desert of popular culture to slake the great thirst of seekers. Among the ones that I admire, and turn to for sustenance and inspiration, are edifying podcasts such as Krista Tippett's *On Being* and Godspeed Institute or questing, interfaith journals such as *The Sun, Parabola, Tikkun, Tiferet, Sufi,* as well as many others.

Yet, since we cannot step into the same river twice, what *does* a return to religion look like? There remain, of course, poets, writers, and artists who pursue direct paths to God through their art. Similarly, there are readers, myself included, who study the lives and utterances of traditional saints and mystics for moral guidance and uplift.

Brad Gooch's biography, *Rumi's Secret* (Harper, 2017) is a fine example of this genre. In his "Secret," the celebrated mystical poet and the world he lived in (around eight hundred years ago) come to life, and we develop a deeper appreciation of why this Muslim saint matters to us so much at our historical moment. Gooch, in conversation with respected Rumi translator Jawid Mojaddedi, quotes Mojaddedi as saying to him: "Rumi resonates, today because people are thinking post-religion. He came to see mysticism as the divine origin of every religion."

Nowadays, there is also a more ambiguous literature (as well as audience) that finds it needless to define their nameless yearning and sees no contradiction in drawing on different traditions to make a patchwork quilt of their inchoate longing. This peculiarly modern pilgrim, unencumbered by dogma, is unembarrassed to treat organized religions as an archaeological site to be excavated for durable ruins—unearthing fragments of Beauty, Grace, Wisdom wherever they might find them and leaving behind what does not resonate, spiritually.

In such literature that is not directly religious, all sorts of spirits are invited, random relics were thrown into the spiritual pot to prepare a nourishing bone broth. Amid the clamor of the culture wars dominating the headlines and airwaves, prayerful prose or poetry and mystic art grant us the opportunity to share Good News and *make a joyful noise.*

One way of doing so is by giving thanks, even in the midst of suffering, or "try[ing] to praise the mutilated world" (Adam Zagajewski). In a hymn of a poem, "Brief for the Defense," Jack Gilbert urges:

> We must have
> the stubbornness to accept our gladness in the ruthless
> furnace of this world. To make injustice the only
> measure of our attention is to praise the Devil.

Belief, in the midst of chaos, remembers the Indestructible world (and we are fearless once we recall that we are, ultimately, deathless). Belief, also teaches us to deeply trust, in spite of appearances, in the innate and inexhaustible goodness of life and how we might contribute to it by caring for our souls. Instinctively, out of self-preservation in the encroaching darkness, we seek out the light with greater urgency—recognizing the necessity for transformation, re-evaluation of values, evolution…

We are called to sanctify our days, in the phrasing of Kahlil Gibran:

> Your daily life is your temple, and your religion
> Whenever you enter into it take with you your all.

Thus, literature in the service of belief, though mindful of other disciplines, is also shrewdly aware of their inadequacies—how the consolations of psychology, philosophy, science, even language cannot quite address the mysteries of the human heart. Mystical art addresses a profound, mute center in us, initiating us into hardly communicable secrets, numinous states of being, and a knowing (gnosis) at the very limits of our self or ego. Our metaphysical eyes are expert at collapsing distances, that way, seeing through the apparent to the Infinite.

Increasingly, I'm intrigued by the idea of artists as mystics and the worship of beauty as a form of prayer. How, for instance, in Omar Khayyam's deceptively simple utterance, 'I pray by admiring a rose,' one finds the connection among the visible, invisible, and indivisible laid bare. Theologian and Sufi mystic Al Ghazali put it thus: "This visible world is a trace of that invisible one, and the former follows the latter like a shadow."

One year before his death, we find the great poet of longing, Rilke, meditating upon the inseparability of the material and spiritual worlds in these memorable, numinous words:

> It was within the power of the creative artist to build a bridge between two worlds, even though the task was almost too great for a man…Everywhere transience is plunging into the depths of Being. It is our task to imprint this temporary, perishable earth into ourselves, so deeply, so painfully and passionately, that its essence can rise again, invisible, inside of us. We are the bees of the invisible. We wildly collect the honey of the visible, to store it in the great golden hive of the invisible.

Reverence for the visible world is not in opposition to the invisible one; in the same way that it is through the body, we access the life of the spirit. Remembering that we are "bees of the invisible" sweetens the suffering and even cheats death of its ultimate sting. We are saved by the very idea of a back and forth, between a here and There.

Through myth and parable, the defiant muse instructs us in the art of being present and then how to vanish without a trace. Poetry explores these variations on the time-honored themes: loss, ecstasy, home, negotiating how best to live with our unquenchable thirst, using odes to joy and manuals of love. Yes, the essence of this art of living is, always, Love…

For some years, I've been meditating on publishing a volume of prayerful writing, a sort of unconscious spiritual autobiography, and have sifted through my books and notes for what might sustain and inspire others. May this modest harvest that you hold in your hands, now, be of some service.

Poems

# Learning to Pray

Long susceptible to the pious heresies,
of mystics, martyrs and other fanatics
mad enough to confound themselves
with G_d, and declare it free of ego

Those spiritually reckless creatures
contemptuous of all rule books,
traffic signs and speeding tickets
in such a hurry were they to arrive

No social drinkers, these revelers
they drank to get drunk, alone
that they might stay that way
—sobriety being the only sin

But what of us without stamina
for such superhuman attention
or the patience to stand in line
inching towards the checkout

Might we forge our own language
(until we can speak in tongues)
by asking of our every action
does this, or that, please You?

# Breath

Beneath the intricate network of noise
there's a still more persistent tapestry
woven of whispers, murmurs and chants

It's the heaving breath of the very earth
carrying along the prayer of all things:
trees, ants, stones, creeks and mountains alike

All giving silent thanks and remembrance
each moment, as a tug on a rosary bead
while we hurry past, heedless of the mysteries

And, yet, every secret *wants* to be told
every shy creature to approach and trust us
if only we patiently listen, with all our senses.

# Oceanside Epiphany

Stepping outside, it's not precisely sun we're after
or the illusion of perfect stillness, but something else
that has to do with the distant riot of children at play
staccato squeals accompanied by the cries of gulls

Or the gentler song of slighter, winged creatures
circling above, frolicking, or pecking at the earth
while the patter of water offers its liquid paean,
and winds tease trees till they shudder with pleasure

This is the quiet pageant we longed to be part of
setting aside our book or papers to vaguely register
ourselves, easing into the pattern, our breath deepening
and our heart slows beating in unison with other things.

# Ramadan

month of quiet strength
and loud weaknesses

when our stubborn habits
and discarded resolutions

are re-examined under the regard
and rigorous slowness of fasting

testing our appetite
for transfiguration

month of waiting and wading
through the shallows to the Deep.

# Desert Revisited

under a whirling skirt of sky
streaming light and stars
groping for that tremendous hem
gingerly over quicksand

as though steadied
beneath some tongue and dissolving
not the absence of sound
but the presence of silence

or, as if transfixed
by a gaze, stern-serene
surveying a dream
foreign-familiar

incorruptible starting point
inviolable horizon
where eye and mind are free
to meditate perfection

there, begin to uncover
buried in dust and disinterest
the immutable letter
(first of the alphabet) *Alif*

under the ever-watchful eye:
fearsome sun, forgiving moon
bless the magnificent hand
all else is blasphemy, a lie

experience quietude
the maturity of ecstasy
longing to utter
the unutterable name

only striving supreme or pure
can ever hope to endure
the absolute face
the awesome embrace.

# Allegiances

I am Destiny's son
loyal by his side
(I never wander long)

Life is as remote to me
as Destiny is intimate:
an ache sweet and serene

When anxious, he gathers me in
promising otherworldly allure
outside all specificity

I honor him in all things
and he follows me everywhere
with eyes dark and tender

Surefooted and steady
threading through trees
I tread his black woods

In his night, I walk in light
in the dawning of understanding
and centered in his gravity.

# Embracing, We Let Go

Perhaps, we are negotiating
not just with one, but always two
—who share the same soil, it is true—
one who lives, another who is dying

A shift in balance begins to take place
once a love of silence is confessed
its roots run deep, its shade a world
and her fruits impossible to forget

From the first, we surrender something
and, gradually, consent to be emptied
transfixed by so much soundless music
drunk and sated through lipless mouths

What use to name this silent master
preparing us for dying or the Divine
(I'm not sure there is a difference)
but know in embracing, we let go.

# Resting Place

There are no maps for the land
my mind's eye is fixed upon
Instead a trail of wrecked ships
mark this treacherous path

My guide, a mysterious star
whose light dims if, briefly,
I happen to turn away—
and which glows brighter
when my heart's aflame.

# Arrivals

I don't quite know how it occurred
that this great fish has appeared
almost fully formed, it seemed
to crowd out all else in my aquarium

Perhaps, this creature of the depths
always was, just out of sight
secretly feeding on hidden longing
and now demands acknowledging

With the swish of a majestic tail
it's upset my incidental decor—
gone the rubber diver and plastic treasure.
The glass frame itself can't be far behind...

# Kneeling in Stages

Twenty years ago, a mighty spirit
whispered to me and rearranged my days
Drink, it said, of solitude; taste of silence
I did as told and it left me a writer

Now, it's back again with grander designs
to rewrite my soul or transform my being
Renounce, it insists, both word and world games
and I have no choice but to submit and bow.

# Summary

The hands were made to clasp
the knees designed to bend
the body created to pray.

*What else is there to say?*

The mouth was shaped to gasp
the eyes drawn to attend
the soul commanded to obey.

*What else is there to say?*

The memory was wired to lapse
the heart fashioned to rend
the will inclined to betray

*What else is there to say?*

# The Light-Keepers

Hope is a lighthouse
(or, at least, a lamppost)
someone must keep vigil
to illumine this possibility

In the dark, a poet will climb
narrow, unsteady stairs
to gaze past crashing waves
and sing us new horizons

Others, less far-sighted, might
be deceived by the encroaching night
mistake the black for lasting, but
not those entrusted with trimming wicks

Their tasks are more pressing—
winding clockworks, replenishing oil—
there is no time for despair
when tending to the Light.

# Hope

Hope's not quite as it seems,
it's slimmer than you'd think
and less steady on its feet

Sometimes, it's out of breath
can hardly see ahead
and cries itself to sleep

It may not tell you all this
or the times it cheated death
but, if you knew it, you'd know

how Hope can keep a secret.

# Reaching

Yes, my Other, this is how
I, always, recognize you:
Upward-reaching and glad,
within wing's wind of a Great Song.

# Corona Verses

We can't simply return to how we were after a crisis—
our homes have become cocoons for radical transformation

Others lives, we finally realize, depend on us and vice versa,
either we change our ways, now, or perish alone-together...

And, if we survive, we might ask of this benevolent master:
Tell us, what new fast can we add to our days ahead?

The same way that Lent or Ramadan are spiritual reminders,
we should consider what sacrifice this pandemic asks of us.

What extreme limit have we reached, or trespassed?
As Laozi says: "Turning back is how the Way moves."

Don't bemoan your four walls; give thanks, for necessary isolation
and pray to emerge from this chrysalis into a new consciousness.

# I Get It, Now

Reviewing the drama of my life
sometimes, I pause and wonder
was this or that incident intended
for my enjoyment or torment?

How about this or that person
do they represent pleasure or pain?
And I smile, bitter-sweetly
knowing, at heart, that one cannot

see anything in isolation…
Angels wrestle with demons
in an eternal dance
for our betterment.

# 3 More Months

"The only unbearable thing is that nothing is unbearable"
said poet Rimbaud, predicting our pandemic

The quarantine was extended, and amid the daily news
of our dying old habits, tentatively, new ones were born

Mysteriously, the forecasted apocalypse never arrived
As months slipped into years, our fears grew tired and fled

Somehow, we were transformed. Not radically, as we had hoped.
But sufficiently so that we might adjust to this new reality.

We lived differently, modestly—expecting less
of others and more of ourselves. Soon, we could no longer imagine

how it was before…the only catastrophe was memory
of our previous unconsciousness

We vowed, *never, again.* But, we forgot
and, eventually, forgave ourselves.

# Never Retreating

a poet stands
trusting on frontlines
ready for martyrdom
risking infection
with the virus
of their age

she examines herself
erupting in flames
or forming antibodies
battling disease
growing stronger
to heal others.

# Lamentations

Write me a book
of lamentations
passionate and profound
pure expressions

of loss and longing
and you will discover
true sorrow is sacred
and your songs are psalms.

# Transportation

When beside yourself, blindfolded and bundled off
where all is winking confidences, suffused smiles
and a sense of imminent revelation
—a state as delineated as a planet—
here the mind's eye must no longer squint
for symbols embedded in the day

the trick is not to steal from this capital of riches
but to cultivate organs of appreciation
breathe the pregnant, wriggling air
acquire a taste for the return and
above all, remember the Way...

# Words

Words are like days:
coloring books or pickpockets,
signposts or scratching posts,
fakirs over hot coals.

Certain words must be earned
just as emotions are suffered
before they can be uttered
—clean as a kept promise.

Words as witnesses
testifying their truths
squalid or rarefied
inevitable, irrefutable.

But, words must not carry
more than they can
it's not good for their backs
or their reputations.

For, whether they dance alone
or with an invisible partner,
every word is a cosmos
dissolving the inarticulate.

# Two of Us

There is the wounded one
maimed, vicious and grasping
Then, there's the Other
invincible and, at times,
lending a steadying hand.

# What If

If he truly believed in angels
they would appear, I said in a dream
(of whom I spoke I can't recall)

Then I remember disintegrating
into hot tears as I realized
that I also spoke of myself

And in that wild, greedy moment
I challenged an angel to appear
as I cowered in a darkened closet

Full of longing and terror, I endured
the suspense of that great *What If*
—relieved the angel did not answer.

# Taut

Between the real
and the Ideal
rejecting one
rejected by the Other

Rack of extremes
the slightest touch
and I reverberate
awful music.

# Awakening from a Dream

In the night, the feathery fists came raining down
He ducked and staggered as they landed, again and again,
On his head, neck and across his shaking back
There was no avoiding this relentless retribution

Could it be, these were the familiar hands of his angels
The same strong ones that, throughout his wrong life,
Carried him through innumerable hardships
Cushioning him from nearly crushing falls

The blows continued to hammer down and he ceased
Trying to avoid what he knew to be his due
Accrued through dismissed warnings and failed promises
He could begin to hear the beating of wings, now

Recognizing, with slow wonder, these fans were also his own
They flapped, like weak devotions, in the dark to shield him
Accompanied by intermittent flashes of a soft blue light
Illuminating the proud army of his divine tormentors.

# Since

I have lost my silences
I have lost my Voice...
peddling an Eternal currency
in life's bustling marketplace
irrepressible song springs up
and is strangled, unsung.

# Turning on the Faucet

What harrowing reproaches
from the depths delivered
with world historic accent

As though clearing a throat
spoiled by long use or disuse
to bewail an ancient crime

Cries of wrathful deities
growling hungry howls
of cavernous cravings

Or, strange pathos echoing
memory's dizzy playground
in plaintive desert threnody

Such sighs of fearful spirits in limbo
somehow unliving and undying
wandering in the land of shades

Startled from much dreamed of sleep
hollows aching, with arthritic creak
into reluctant and rusty service

What weird music from breathing flutes:
moving water, steel and air entreaties.
Oh, that sublime singing of the pipes!

Sublime in the sense Milton meant it
"the beauty that hath terror in it."

# The Opposite of Virtue

One might say, a vice is a vise
never mind if metal or moral,
it's basically the same device

With cunning moveable jaws
designed to fix us in place
and cheat us of a chance at grace

Impervious to all advice, habit
hotly whispers false reassurance
while tightening its iron grip

It takes no effort to slip into vice,
but virtue is trickier to stick to
like the back of a bucking bronco.

# The Art of Storm-Riding

I could not decipher the living riddle of my body
put it to sleep when it hungered, and overfed it
when time came to dream

I nearly choked on the forked tongue of my spirit
between the real and the ideal, rejecting the one
and rejected by the other

I still have not mastered that art of storm-riding
without ears to apprehend howling winds
or eyes for rolling waves

Always the weather catches me unawares, baffled
by maps, compass, stars and the entire apparatus
of bearings or warning signals

Clutching at driftwood, eyes screwed shut, I tremble
hoping the unhinged night will pass and I remember
how once I shielded my flame.

# Drylands

Tell me, have you found a sea
deep enough to swim in
deep enough to drown in

waters to engage you
distract you, keep you
from crossing to the other shore?

# Night Bird

How night descends, enveloping us in its great sacred wings,
with the promise of a deeper silence than day dared to offer
Now, if only we can endure this tremendous stillness
we might still be restored to ourselves, once again
Tread lightly, cover the smiling mirrors and sullen screens
don't let any spirit escape through the 1,001 trap doors

Listen, those are your own footsteps you hear approaching

Don't look around, or move much, enemies of the holy hush
crouch nearby, ready to pounce. They want your attention
in pieces, smashed like a porcelain vase. The quiet majesty
of your mounting wholeness disturbs them more than anything else
Try, try with all your might, to make it last the night. As you
tremble
and sweat, remember this triumph next time you forsake your
oaths.

# Afterthought

and, when we pass are we caught
in the pockets of afterlife
—the sorted and unsorted—

or, do we continue slipping
through a fault in the lining
through the gaps in space?

# Start, Again

Sunset is a gentle master to all that are stricken
patiently, teaching us how to melt a bruise away
Watch how, with a silver whisk, that cracked egg
of a setting sun is majestically stirred, and put to rest

Violent violet, pining pink, and yelling yellow
all agitated, then muted, their differences reconciled
Until all that remains is a faint tattoo of quiet hurt
pearlescent wisps of smoke from a sighing flame

that night, stealthily, smothers and hushes away…

# What the Sunset Said

Something happened as the light was dying
it wasn't just post-coital exhalation
where the once-possessed body is used up
and all that remains is bodiless trance

Rather, it seemed they were mirroring
a preternatural stillness,
two spiritual sentinels
transfixed and somehow Other

Science calls it "twilight calibrated magnetic compass"
yet it appeared beyond mere direction-finding
more a kind of existential orientation
consolidating all they knew, and listening

with their entire being, participating
silently, in a universal hymn
until they were pulled, as out of a viscous substance,
by the hungry cry of their nearby young

to become two feral pigeons, again
with this-world considerations
parenting, foraging, keeping alive
and, dazed, they consented to their stations.

# I Ran

I ran hard and far
to outdistance my pain
But, when I got lost
my pain found me—
caressed me, wordlessly
and carried me Home.

# Two Types of Kisses

What is a mystic
but one who swoons,
defenseless
in the face of beauty

A natural believer
in evolution of spirit.

Two types of kisses,
and the choice is yours:
either with burning lips,
that bind and blind

Or a lipless kind,
preparing us to leave
a too-tight skin behind.

I stand, helpless, before
the sensuality of stretches,
but get down on bended knee
for the spiritual variety.

# Holy Mess

Overnight, your once blessed existence
might reverse course
become an alien thing
and you stand accused
of unspeakable crimes

Never mind, you are innocent
of these base horrors—
as Kafka says, in his *Trial,*
"Guilt is never to be doubted"

Be grateful, then
there are still dreadful sins
in our fallen world
of which you are blameless

So, tell me, how will this crucible
change you? Now, show how this
unasked-for crisis is
blessing, allow it to assist
the birth of your longed-for self

Thank God, for this Holy Mess!

# What the Migraine Said

As I lie, here, half in and out of consciousness
I imagine my migraine as a world migraine
my cluster headache as a cluster of world aches
that we must tip toe around like a sleeping tiger

The sleep of reason produces monsters—
this we know from art and the news:
murder and sham leaders shooting themselves
in one foot and chewing on the other.

But, the sleep of reason produces angels, also
like Love, which is no whimsical thing,
a love like bull, bullfighter and bloody cape,
billowing in the wind, like an open heart

Beckett said this best, truth in paradox:
*The mystics I like...their burning illogicality*
*—the flame...Which consumes all our filthy logic...*
Where there are demons there is something precious

Once we know this, the rest is silence.
The master is not permitted
the same mistakes of a novice.

# Seasoning

From time to time
a lick of flame
tasted him

testing to see
if he might be
salty and sweet

for all Eternity…
if he was ready
to exit the pit.

# Secrets

Can we ever write about secrets
that we cannot speak of
the thing or two that determine
who we are and what we do

When can we hint at the harm
we've hardly survived
the realization that our allure
is due to deformity

Sure, we confess in code
here, there and everywhere
beneath our breath
and over their heads

But when can we ever speak,
plainly, of our obscene pain
to whom and how might we
unburden ourselves, artlessly

The answer might be *never*
whispers art, to which we owe all
—our lives, wisdom and masks—
only transformation will set us free.

# 11<sup>th</sup> Hour Plea

One foot here, one foot there
how much longer, weary pilgrim,
lingering at the threshold?

One step forward, two steps back
—still lusting after this world—
Have you forgotten your promises?

To die to your self, to transmute
the mud to gold, to surrender
distractions and consent to be born?

# Bargaining with Whom?

The price we pay
for exquisite secrets
is exorbitant

In private rooms,
we are fleeced.

Far from the madding crowd
at the bazaar, there we are,
sheepish and sly

Seeking to strike a deal
but with…Whom?

A gem-like truth
is up for auction
for those with diamond hearts

To kiss a mystery,
a miracle to hoard

Naturally, is well beyond
what we ever dreamed
we could afford

We give our lives for such
shuddering intimacies

And hope and pray
our lives will be enough,
the balance cancelled

The guardian of the riddle
must only speak in riddles.

# Truth in Advertising

morning epiphany
applicable to love and life
in haiku-like purity:

only freshly squeezed
separation is natural
shake well to enjoy!

*In fructose veritas.*

# Dawning

There are hours when every thing creaks
when chairs stretch their arms, tables their legs
and closets crack their backs, incautiously

Fed up with the polite fantasy
of having to stay in one place
and stick to their stations

Humans too, at work, or in love
know such aches and growing pains
when inner furnishings defiantly shift

As decisively, and imperceptibly, as a continent
some thing will stretch, croak or come undone
so that everything else must be reconsidered

One restless dawn, unable to suppress the itch
of wanderlust, with a heavy door left ajar
semi-deliberately, and a new light teasing in

Some piece of immobility will finally quit
suddenly nimble on wooden limbs
as fast as a horse, fleeing the stable.

# Misread Signs

False prophet, nightly heralding a man-made god
gilding the air with promise of revelation
a song, in truth, no less sweet for being counterfeit,
let us forgive the short-sighted visionary

Pity the poor bird its ill-timed enthusiasm,
its unholy lapse of judgment and misplaced hymn
having mistaken a common streetlamp
for the miracle of a rising sun…

# Colors

To start with, saints are brown
like everything around

Then blue, from trying
the fine art of dying

At last, they're lavender
the color of surrender.

# Poy

He plays with fire
against the night sky
he looks like a man
juggling the stars

Now, humbly bowing
harnessing elements
the chains mystically dissolve
and only the dance remains

Slow dancing the figure whirls
like a Sufi in a skirt of flame
or some spiritual bullfighter
with his twisting cape ablaze

Until amid luminous circus wheels
the flame ritual dies out
trailing a numinous light
like esoteric script across the night.

# I Saw My Face

I saw my face this morning
hovering at the base
of a coffee cup

eyes liquid black
and thirsting
lips parted as if

some great spoon
had stirred me to the depths
and left everything, swirling.

# You, Again

You again, of the singing wound
here again, lost and found and lost
trafficking in metaphysics and eternity
as the nearest hopes

where to, pilgrim
outdistancing chasms
rationing emotions
seeking sustenance

for the self too subtle and proud
for words
nocturnal flower, nurtured solitude
watered night

there you go, restraining the impulse
to say it all at once
even surrounded by silence
still filled with noise

now, having stirred some thrumming
hour when the moon throws
her full-bodied light
over all, like a silver screen night
of silent films, the whirring
of the reel.

# St. Sebastian

Sometimes, he found it difficult
to dislodge the arrows—
preferring to keep them there
reverberating in silence
along with his invisible wounds.

## Interstices

My hours are afraid of my days
mistrust placing their feet down
suspicious of finding a foothold
*tic toc* they tip toe, self-consciously

My days are afraid of my years
never able to forget themselves
standing around as I try to sleep
shifting their weight, shuffling fears

In the interstices, it is timeless
unwound and happily unfound
there we slip through the sieve
between those immeasurable spaces…

# Unentitled

I have not found the key to myself
the one that will get the high gates
to swing wide open and the lights
to come on, at once

When not denied entrance entirely
I fumble in the dark and stumble
blindly, run into doors and walls
groping and hoping

I knock my head against false ceilings
and trip on traps I forgot to remember
then start at the sight of my reflection
bumping into myselves.

# Mystery of Doors

Every jammed door has its trick
how much pressure to apply
where to push, just so, how deep
at what angle to jiggle, pull out

So, too, with the apparently
difficult doors of opportunity
that stubbornly balk at all rattling
yet, suddenly, yield at the key moment.

# Starlings

Hypnotic like a school of airborne fish
they frolic about in the open sky
flickering into focus and diffusing
back to the ether that spawned them

Gathering like a storm and breaking in waves
raining hard, a downpour of butterflies
flitting like a great kite, giddy it got away
yet guided by a steady and invisible hand

How do they know to spell such exalted shapes
fluid arabesques across the stage of heaven
as they swarm and glide as though of one mind
a soundless symphony, mysteriously conducted?

# Mystic, Misfit

These are the wandering years.

Born exile,
homeless at last
tormenting idea
become beckoning reality

Lover of longing's song
and whispered promises
all the colors once fixed
now, profusely bleed

Just as constellations disperse
the pattern no longer discernible
here, within reach, the future looms
high as imagination, deep as fear

*Yes,* these are the wandering years…

# Morning

Every day, regardless
of the night's previous
sulks or arguments,

morning climbs into bed
breathless as a child
eager to play.

Will you rise
in the same vein
to greet this challenge?

## Poet Try

set aside your imperiled existence
cowering before a heartless idea
prostrate before a heartless ideal
spiritual asthmatic, straining for prophesy

verse versatile yet word weary
continue picking the teeth of things
loosening meaning with words, amid
writhing writing and growing pains

trust in longing to sing itself
ushering you to the horizon
of your hopes

Poet try

and endure
your Wisdom
gently mocking

Till the soil
until the soul
erupts in flower.

# Fine, Tuning

Whatever else artists might be
—monsters, angels, prophets,
battlegrounds or burial grounds—
they are also tuning forks;
struck at every turn and
sounding out the worlds.

# Gradual Escape

In the mirror, old age is peering through
my features grow more distant, indistinct
—blurring the iron bars of personality.

I'm being hollowed out, I feel it
in the subtle droop of skin and will
Like the life stuffing were slowly
being spooned from me

My mind, too, is being emptied
of needless concerns
(such as, who's in charge)
traveling lighter, demanding less

One day, I'll finally slip out this
loosening body bag
Simply sling it over the shoulder
of my sturdy spirit.

# Gestation

This long disorientation,
I, now, better understand;
as my soul is rewritten
I have been learning
how to walk (on air)
and breathe (underwater).

It's best not to say too much
or think you know anything;
preferable to keep very still
lest you spoil the process
—when you are being reborn.

Gestation is hardly time
for grand pronouncements:
lie low, feed, listen for clues.
Grow, inwardly, in knowing
before declaring it to the world.

# Aphorisms

Learn to recognize those who wish you success, versus those who long for your ruin. Then, you will better understand the ways of G_d and devil.

*

We have only to falter for sins to commit themselves.

*

The punishment fits the sin—even when we are wrongly accused.

*

Let he who is without sin complain about injustice.

The starved think differently than the sated.

*

Gains obtained, unethically, are short-lived—even if they last a lifetime.

*

Always act as if you are being watched: where the surveillance state and spiritual state agree.

*

In the same way that love is regenerative medicine, hate is a degenerative disease.

Our insecurities prevent us from recognizing how dearly we are Beloved.

*

Love has many faces—righteous indignation is one of them.

*

If we ask life for favors, we must be prepared to return them.

*

Remember, no one can help you, but—through Him, alone—anyone can lend a hand.

You cannot ask for Help, then shun it every time it arrives.

*

Looking a gift horse in the mouth is the human condition.

*

Miracles are proud creatures—they reveal themselves only to those who Believe.

*

So long as you trust in anything else, the miracle shall be withheld.

Logical interpretations are the Miracle's modesty.

*

The guardian of the riddle must speak in riddles.

*

To acquire a third eye, one cannot blink.

*

Trust in longing to sing itself.

One's self must die in the delivery room, to give birth to God.

*

In the spiritual dimension, versus the merely literary, one cannot produce a masterpiece before they become one.

*

One definition of success might be: refining our appetites, while deepening our hunger.

*

It's not sacrifice, unless we give up what we love.

In critical circumstances, the difference between success and failure, health and sickness, even life and death, is a matter of stamina and sacrifice.

*

To live heedlessly, while still in harm's way, is to court disaster.

*

It's easier to be fearless, when we remember we are deathless.

*

We can lend ideas our breath, but Ideals require our entire lives.

All who are tormented by an Ideal must learn to make an ally of failure.

*

The path to Peace is littered with dead selves.

*

Our salvation lies on the other side of our gravest danger.

*

Our fascination with the monstrous perpetuates it.

Every Messiah is reluctant—at least, initially.

*

All languages are rough translations of our native tongue: Spirit.

*

Poems are like bodies—a fraction of their power resides in their skin. The rest belongs to the spirit that swims through them.

*

When we think we are stealing from life's fleeting pleasures, we are stealing from our own Eternal Joy.

Paths are also relationships—to be meaningful, they require fidelity.

*

Tell me, can you tell the difference between bed bugs and the bite of conscience?

*

Every time we betray our conscience, we strangle an angel. Yet, it's not certain we are allotted an infinite supply of winged pardons.

*

Unheeded pricks of conscience might return as harpoons of circumstance.

As in the physical realm, so in the spiritual: it takes one moment of inattention to slip and fall.

*

If we pay attention, we are ushered along our path in winks and nudges.

*

Aphorisms respect the wisdom of silence by disturbing it, briefly.

*

Chasing silence is like embarking on a whale hunt. If one catches up with this creature of the depths, there is the danger of being swallowed whole.

Pity atheists their pitilessness. They are like persons hurt in love, who vow: *Never, again.*

*

Miracles are everyday occurrences, recognizing them is not.

*

Our most profound prayers hardly reach our lips; they are made with our entire being.

*

At the heart of every vice sits selfishness, yawning.

What we refer to as 'the real world' is often our failure of imagination.

*

We're here to pass around the ball of light, while keeping our fingerprints off it.

*

No matter how we dream or scheme, being born is always a surprise.

*

The ascetic does not deny pleasure; he shuns the coarse, in favor of the exalted.

The ascetic ideal speaks, thus: indulge, and forego Vision.

*

Spiritual fast food leads to spiritual indigestion.

*

Art for art's sake is a dead end; art for heart's sake is the way out.

*

Said a poem to a poet: Can I trust you? Is your heart pure to carry me, are your hands clean to pass me on?

From what you have, create what you have not—the poem teaches the poet.

*

When the life of a poet is a poem, the poet becomes a mystic.

*

Numbness is a spiritual malady; true detachment its opposite.

*

You can't bury pain and not expect it to grow roots.

If we care for ourselves, we may turn our pain into gifts for others.

*

If we do not care for our souls, we become a burden for others.

*

If there is someone we might ask forgiveness of, then there is no one we can deny forgiveness to.

*

We steal from ourselves when we share an idea, or feeling, before it has ripened.

*

Integrity is to live in a house built by words.

Why announce to the world your few good deeds, when you hide your many bad ones—even from yourself?

*

To evolve means we've been listening.

*

Just as mysteriously as spiritual favors are granted, so they may also be revoked.

*

Wings are, always, on loan.

If our hearts should harden and turn to ice we must try, at least, not to blame the weather.

*

Unlike prose, poetry can keep its secrets.

*

Poetry is what we say to ourselves, when there's nowhere left to hide.

*

We scramble the first half of our lives to assemble a self; and in the second half, if we are wise, to dismantle it.

Self is a labyrinth, at the heart of which sits Spirit, hoping to be found.

*

Poetry: the native tongue of hysterics—adolescents and mystics, alike.

*

Mysticism is the disappearing act that takes a lifetime.

*

To become a mystic is not impossible; one must only endure being a beggar, mad and dead.

It is possible to subsist entirely on a diet of honey and wine, or poetry and mysticism.

*

Know your Muse, and its diet.

*

When the Muse is silent, confess ignorance.

*

The divided self is spiritually immature. Divine union begins with self unity.

All the unmet promises that we make, to ourselves and others, return to taunt us.

*

Poor rational mind, it would sooner accept a believable lie than an incredible truth.

*

The contemplative life is not a passive one.

*

Compassion is to recognize the role we play in the creation of our enemy.

Every enmity with another is part of our unfinished work on ourselves. A free person has no enemies.

*

The more closely we listen to ourselves, the more likely we are to overhear others.

*

As we make peace with ourselves, we become more tolerant of our faults—in others.

*

See the sun, how it shifts the light of its attention, gradually, from one thing to the next. Be like it, don't fixate.

Each day we cast the net, and only what is ours returns to us.

*

Enter every day with empty hands, trusting you will receive what you need.

*

To anticipate the worst is to contribute towards its realization.

*

Our longings shape our future. Pessimism poisons life and then wonders why it chokes.

The precious few times I peered into my crystal ball, I made out the letters T.R.U.S.T.

*

There is no private life; what we do, in secret, is secreted, publicly.

*

One distinction between diabolical and Divine inspiration is the duration of pleasure it affords.

*

In contrast to goodness, there is something boring about evil; it is finite.

We inhabit a moral universe; amorality is, ultimately, immorality.

*

Between decadence and mysticism, a line as fine as a fissure—the depth of an abyss...

*

To ask *Why Me?* prevents the answer from revealing itself.

*

The paradox of success in life is to be aware of your vices, but not your virtues.

Inspiration speaks in fits and starts—revealing to us only what is necessary, at the time.

*

We have art lest we perish of untruth.

*

If we are willing to sacrifice what is dearest to us, in perfect submission, we discover that we are not required to.

*

There is no respite in the garden without, first, struggle in the wilderness.

A true poet, like a mystic, is not too proud to admit that in matters great and small, they cannot proceed without receiving further instructions.

*

A poem arrives like a hand in the dark.

*

The first step towards Love, the middle and the last, are non-verbal.

*

Fallen angels bleed.

Silence is golden, since it's the native tongue of the Spirit.

*

Vices are dangerous because they lead us to even greater moral injury: heedlessness and hardness of heart.

*

The mysticism of Love unlocks secrets.

*

There's some mysticism in poetry; but, there's poetry in all mysticism.

Mysticism teaches us that if we hold our breath long enough, we can breathe underwater.

*

To mate with the sublime, sublimate.

*

Desire never dies, which is why mystics shrewdly entrusts it to the Eternal.

*

Desire is to the body what longing is to the spirit.

Pleasure might be snatched from life's hands; but joy, like all blessings, must be granted.

*

Every day we are offered this world or the next; but we cannot be myopic and farsighted, at once.

*

Mysticism is a courtship.

*

The best way to spoil any marriage is to speak too often and easily of it; this is true of faith. Love and work grow strong in secret soil.

In serving words, faithfully, we also serve one another.

*

Radical humility: to entertain the possibility that our worst detractors might be right.

*

Conscience says: time wasted polishing the sheath, should be spent sharpening the sword.

*

Maybe, crises are self-induced, a last-ditch effort we gift ourselves to, finally, transform.

We have rituals because we are forgetful by nature. Books are another way to remember what we know.

*

Strange, the power of the past—how our spiritual ancestors become our future masters.

*

To accept this world as it is isn't realistic; it's cynical.

*

Hope is another name for refusing to accept things as they are.

Cynicism's knowingness cheats itself out of true knowing.

*

Cynics are in need of constant reassurance; first, that their worst doubts about humanity are true and then, of course, that they are not.

*

In the deep end, every stroke counts.

*

Laws: civil disobedience, sometimes, but always spiritual obedience.

*

The person who knows how to accept will taste a hidden sweetness even in suffering.

*

Accept the calamity and the burden is lifted.

*

Silence is the great jeweler of words—certifying their authenticity and assessing their worth.

*

When in doubt, meditate upon your wound.

If, as Rumi says, 'the wound is the place where the Light enters,' we must keep our wound clean.

*

To write is to bow is to pray.

*

You cannot hear another, while you are speaking. It's the same with the Divine. Listen.

*

If religion is recognized as organized Love then hate, by definition, is heresy. An angry prayer is a contradiction in terms.

## About the Author

Yahia Lababidi, Egyptian-Lebanese, is the author of eight books of poetry and prose; most recently, the collection of essays and conversations, *Revolutions of the Heart* (Wipf and Stock, 2020). Nominated for a Pushcart Prize, three times, Lababidi's writing has been translated into several languages, and he has participated in international poetry festivals throughout the USA and Europe, as well as the Middle East.

# Advance Praise

Lababidi's new volume brings a dynamic flow to his subject that is both timeless and very contemporary; his insights summon us to a spiritual but entirely undogmatic journey.

—Abdal Hakim Murad, author of *Travelling Home* and Dean of Cambridge Muslim College

*Learning to Pray* is a masterpiece. Yahia Lababidi is a lyrical genius touched by the genies. I wonder how he is able, time after time, to work such miracles--authentic and truly beautiful.

—Peter Zsoldos, Ambassador of the Slovak Republic and poetry translator

Despite its insistence that the mystic "swoons, / defenseless / in the face of beauty," the real mysticism of Lababidi's *book of longing* is not private but shared: the speaker swoons, and leaves the reader defenseless in the face of beauty.

—H. L. Hix, American poet, academic and editor

In lean, luminescent verse, Lababidi has created a portal into quiet worlds, guiding us to be our best selves. He reminds us of the richness of the stilled and savored. In difficult times, his poems help the reader to summon courage and beauty.

—Carla Power, author of *Prodigal Son* and former *Newsweek* correspondent